Puppies

A very first picture book

Consultant: Nico...

LORENZ

You *always* have the ball.

Oh no ...
what's that?

But I *want*
to chew it ...

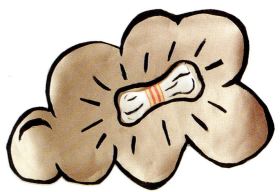

I'm longing
for a bone.

Mmm ... yum, yum!

Finished!

Mum! There's a phone
call for you!

This thing makes noises as well.

This is *my* cushion.

I'm getting off now.

Well *are* we going for a walk or not?

Maybe I'll just chew my
lead instead.

Oh *please* can I come
home with you?

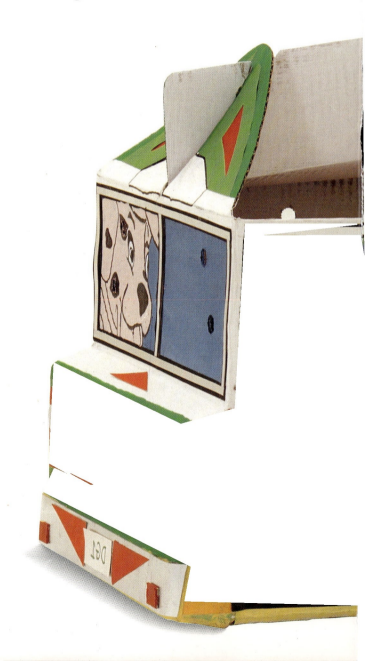

Psst! I think I'm
stuck in this jug.

Being a puppy
is *so* tiring!

First published in 1996 by Lorenz Books

Reprinted in 1998

© Anness Publishing Limited 1996

Lorenz Books is an imprint of
Anness Publishing Limited
Hermes House, 88-89 Blackfriars Road
London SE1 8HA

ISBN 1 85967 124 1

A CIP catalogue record for this book
is available from the British Library

Publisher: Joanna Lorenz
Children's Books Editor: Caroline Beattie
Photographer: Jane Burton
Design and Typesetting:
   Michael Leaman Design Partnership

Printed in Hong Kong/China

10 9 8 7 6 5 4 3 2